MOTOR TRADE
LAW

AN I.M.I. STUDENTS GUIDE
by

Anthea Worsdall, OBE, FIMI, Solicitor
Michael J. Pearce, MIMgt, MIRTE, MBIM
Peter Groves, FIMI, LLB, MA, PhD, Solicitor

First published in 1989 by
The Institute of the Motor Industry
Fanshaws
Brickendon
Hertford
SG13 9PQ
Second edition 1990
Third edition 1991
Fourth edition 1993
Fifth edition 1994
Sixth edition 1995
Revised edition 1998

© 1989 The Institute of the Motor Industry

Printed in Great Britain by
Black Bear Press Ltd
Cambridge

ISBN 1 871880 00 9